FOLENS HISTORY HIGHLIGHTS

History for Juniors 1

Mary Green

Contents

Introduction	3
Archaeology	4
The Celts and the Romans	8
The Anglo-Saxons	12
The Vikings	16
Viking Ships	20
Rich Tudors	24
Poor Tudors	28
Henry VIII	32
The Second World War and the Home Front	36
The Second World War: Evacuation	40
Ancient Egypt	44
Coverage of the QCA Scheme of Work for Key Stages 1 and 2	48

Acknowledgements

Cover picture: Popperfoto.

p.9 Quote from *The British Encyclopaedia*, 1933.

p.27 'Tudor Kitchen', copyright Fotomas Index (UK).

p.30 'Beggar being Whipped', copyright Fotomas Index (UK).

p.37 Illustration by Doreen Debenham from *The Complete Home Entertainer*, published by Odhams Press.

p.38A Quote from Colin Perry, *Boy in the Blitz*, published by Sutton Publishing, 1980.

p.38B Quote from Bill Brandt, *War Work*, exhibition at The Photographer's Gallery, 24 June–3 September 1983.

p.39B Taken from *Children of the Blitz* Copyright © Robert Westall 1995. Reproduced by permission of Macmillan Children's Books, London.

p.41A&B Quotes from Martin Parsons and Penny Starns, *The Evacuation: the true story*, published by DSN (based on the BBC Radio 4 programme, presented by Charles Wheeler, first transmitted in 1999 and produced by Martin Weitz Associates); quotes reproduced by kind permission of DSN.

p46B Illustration based on a picture in Lancelot Hogben, *Man Must Measure The Wonderful World of Mathematics*, published by Rathbone Books, 1955.

© 2002 Folens Limited, on behalf of the author.

United Kingdom: Folens Publishers, Apex Business Centre, Boscombe Road, Dunstable, LU5 4RL.
Email: folens@folens.com

Ireland: Folens Publishers, Greenhills Road, Tallaght, Dublin 24.
Email: info@folens.ie

Poland: JUKA, ul. Renesansowa 38, Warsaw 01-905.

Folens allows photocopying of pages marked 'copiable page' for educational use, providing that this use is within the confines of the purchasing institution. Copiable pages should not be declared in any return in respect of any photocopying licence.

Folens publications are protected by international copyright laws. All rights are reserved. The copyright of all materials in this publication, except where otherwise stated, remains the property of the publisher and author. No part of this publication may be reproduced, stored in a retrieval system, or transmitted, in any form or by any means, for whatever purpose, without the written permission of Folens Limited.

Mary Green hereby asserts her moral rights to be identified as the author of this work in accordance with the Copyright, Designs and Patents Act 1988.

Editor: Jennifer Steele
Layout artists: Suzanne Ward and Patricia Hollingsworth
Cover design: Martin Cross
Illustrations: James Field (SGA Graphic Design & Illustration Agency)

First published 2002 by Folens Limited.
Reprinted 2002.

Every effort has been made to trace the copyright holders of material used in this publication. If any copyright holder has been overlooked, we should be pleased to make any necessary arrangements.

British Library Cataloguing in Publication Data. A catalogue record for this publication is available from the British Library.

ISBN 1 84303 157 4

Introduction

The **History Highlights** series focuses on the revised National Curriculum for History (History 2000) and the QCA scheme of work for Key Stages 1 and 2, and can be used by teachers to help reinforce key skills and provide information. Historical sources are often used and the books will fit easily into existing schemes and materials.

Each book is divided into 11 chapters and covers a wide range of periods. The teacher can, therefore, focus on those chapters that are relevant to his or her curriculum. The chapters are divided into four pages: one *Ideas Page*, one *Resource Page* and two *Activity Pages*. The *Resource* and *Activity Pages* are photocopiable, to be used with the children, while the *Ideas Page* gives guidance for the teacher. It is laid out as follows:

Background
This gives useful information on the chapter and period, helping to place the *Resource Page* and *Activity Pages* within a historical context.

Learning Objectives
The learning objectives detail the specific skills involved in the chapter.

Resource Page
The *Resource Page* can be used by the teacher in discussion with the children at the beginning of the lesson. It focuses on key questions related to the chapter.

Using the Activity Pages
This section outlines the tasks and skills involved. The children can use the *Activity Pages* together or independently, according to age and ability. (It may be felt, for example, that teacher intervention is more appropriate, particularly at Key Stage 1.)

Follow-up
This final section makes suggestions on how the skills or content in each chapter could be developed, for example by using IT or through research work.

Several important historical skills are covered in the books, such as:

At Key Stage 1
- Developing a sense of the passage of time, appreciating that there is a difference between events in the recent and more distant past.
- Identifying with peoples' lives in the past, for example through empathy.
- Recognising that sources from the past can give us information about the past.

At Key Stage 2
- Understanding that the past may have an effect upon the future.
- Identifying the reasons behind events and the consequences of those events.
- Recognising that while some things change, others may stay the same.
- Using chronology and historical language to describe past events.

At the end of the book is a table showing coverage of the QCA scheme of work for Key Stages 1 and 2.

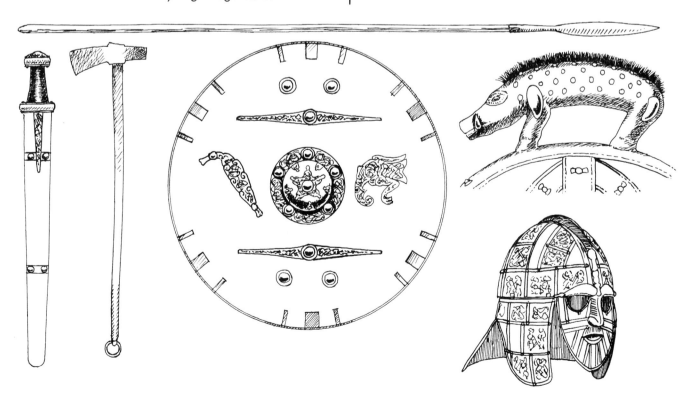

ideas page

Archaeology

Background

Modern archaeological techniques, such as those involved in geophysics (for example, looking beneath the ground using radio waves), give the archaeologist a clearer view of what is under the soil before disturbing it. In consequence, less damage occurs and the 'dig' can proceed with greater care.

Learning Objectives

- To understand the importance of evidence.
- To understand the work of an archaeologist.
- To deduce information from pictures of excavations.

Resource Page

The Dig

The illustration is of an archaeological dig in which the team is carrying out various jobs such as assessing and measuring the site, making searches and labelling and recording artefacts. The children can discuss the illustration in pairs or a small group, and try to reach a consensus about what is happening. Clarify anything that they are uncertain about and point out that:

- different layers of soil will reveal different things
- the spot where an artefact is found is also recorded
- the finds will be sent away to museums and universities to be cleaned and restored.

Using the Activity Pages

Useful Tools

The children are given a list of pictures that represent the basic equipment used by an archaeological team. Working together, they should try to decide what each piece of equipment is for (using the knowledge already gained), and complete the chart. Explain also that adequate preparation of a site is important, not only because an incorrect site might be located, but also because evidence could be damaged.

The Archaeologist

This writing frame should help the children to sum up what they have learned about the work of the archaeologist and its importance in giving us a picture of the past. Useful words that the children should be familiar with are listed at the bottom of the page. Further words can be added if needed. The children might discuss possible notes for each section of the frame before writing their own version.

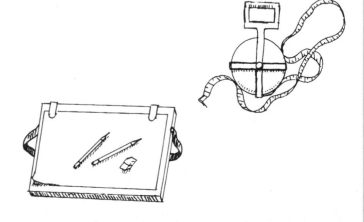

Follow-up

- Discuss other simple means used by archaeologists for finding out information. For example:
  - tree-ring dating tells the age of a tree and can therefore give information about how old wood is
  - analysis carried out on pollen that has survived over time will give an indication of the plants that were growing in and around an archaeological site.

The Dig

Archaeologists are like detectives. Their work is to discover what happened in the past. They do this by looking at where people used to live. So most of their work is digging beneath the soil.

- Look at the excavation below. It is usually called a 'dig'.

Talking and Thinking
- What do you think the people are doing? Look at each one carefully and decide what kind of job they are doing.
- What do you think is in the trays?
- Do you think you could do any of these jobs? What would be the most difficult part?

Useful Tools

Before archaeologists can carry out their work they must find out where to dig and record what the site is like. When the dig begins, anything that is found is labelled and recorded.

- Below are some of the tools an archaeologist uses. Write down what you think each one is used for.

Tools	Use

Other tools that archaeologists might use are a toothbrush, a soft paintbrush, a sieve and a riddle (a coarse sieve).

The Archaeologist

- Complete the writing frame below. Use the words at the bottom to help you.

Archaeologists are people who
_____
_____
_____

An archaeological dig is
_____
_____
_____

The jobs carried out at the dig are very skilful because
_____
_____
_____
_____

and also because
_____
_____
_____

When a find is discovered the archaeologist will
_____
_____
_____

investigate   excavation   site
equipment   label   record   artefact

ideas page
The Celts and the Romans

Background

The Celtic culture had developed in what is now central Europe by around 750BC. The Celtic tribes came to inhabit much of the British Isles, parts of Asia Minor and much of Europe, developing a sophisticated culture noted for the quality of its metalwork. They also had an established religion and were expert charioteers. They were not as skilled in battle as the Romans (they seem to have fought more as individuals than as a team), and by 54BC, the well-organised army of Julius Caesar had brought many of the Celtic tribes under Roman rule. However, Celtic culture was not obliterated by Roman settlement. Although the Romans dominated, often cruelly, the two cultures did co-exist and were both influenced by each other. The Romans assimilated some Celtic beliefs and there was also some intermarriage.

Learning Objectives

- To understand who the Celts and the Romans were.
- To recognise that Celtic culture was sophisticated.
- To recognise that evidence can be conflicting.
- To recognise that the Celts and Romans mixed and sometimes intermarried.

Resource Page

The Celts

'The Celts' Resource Page provides a variety of information about the Celts and how they were perceived by the Romans. The children should study the sources carefully and use them to answer the questions. The last two questions are the most important and the children need to understand that Celtic culture was complex and did not disappear when the Romans arrived.

Using the Activity Pages

Family Life

Although this may not be typical of family life at the time (family life varied with social status), it is useful to show the children that Celts and Romans mixed, as people from different cultures do today. They should be able to identify the different Celtic and Roman dress, Celtic jewellery, loom and cloth and Roman furniture and mosaic floor.

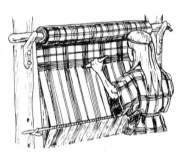

Looking at the Evidence

Here the children are given a writing frame to help them to record what they have learned. They are asked to explain what 'evidence' is and should realise that it can help to build up an accurate historical picture. They also need to know that not all evidence is reliable (such as a Roman's view of the Celts), and may conflict with other evidence (archaeological). The writing frame can be adapted to suit work done on the Romans as well as the Celts. Provide the children with an opportunity to discuss and draft possible notes for each section of the writing frame before they complete their individual piece of writing.

Follow-up

- The children could study the Celts further by looking at the typical Celtic warrior and how Celtic battle dress differed from that of the Romans. They can also include a study of Boudicca and try to decide why the Romans overcame the Celts.
- Some children might investigate Celtic mythology and look at the importance of the Druids. They might investigate why the Romans, who were tolerant of other religions and beliefs, were suspicious of these priests.

The Celts

The Celts lived in Britain before the Romans invaded. They looked very fierce in battle because they painted themselves with woad. This was a blue dye taken from a plant. They also put lime on their hair to make it spiky. Some Romans called them barbarians, and thought their homes and way of life were simple.

Weaving

Celtic pots

Celtic jewellery

The Romans did not expect the Celts to be good charioteers.

> The Britons [Celts] were excellent metal workers and expert in the art of enamelling on bronze.
>
> *The British Encyclopaedia* (1933)

Talking and Thinking
- Why do you think the Celts used woad and made their hair spiky?
- What kinds of things did the Celts make?
- What is a charioteer?
- What views did some Romans have about the Celts?
- Look up the words 'savage' and 'barbarian' in the dictionary.
- What evidence can you find that the Celts were more advanced than the Romans thought they were?
- What do you think happened to the Celts when the Romans came?

Family Life

Sometimes a Roman married a Celt. Sometimes Celts became rich and took on Roman habits and dress. Archaeologists have found that some Roman houses were built where Celtic ones had stood. They think this means that some Celts became more like the Romans.

- Look carefully at the picture below.

- Make a chart and list all the things that are Celtic and Roman in two columns like this:

Roman	Celtic

Looking at the Evidence

- Why do you think we collect evidence and study evidence in History?

We collect and study evidence in History because _____
_____
_____

- What have I learned about the Celts?

I have learned that _____
_____
_____

- We have evidence for this.

The evidence we learned about is _____
_____
_____
_____

Most of this evidence comes from _____
_____
_____

Other evidence comes from _____
_____
_____

Evidence is not always reliable because _____
_____
_____

ideas page

The Anglo-Saxons

Background

The Angles and Saxons first began to journey to the British Isles across the North Sea from what we now call Denmark and Germany towards the end of the Roman Empire. They ruled parts of England from AD449 until the Norman Conquest in 1066, during what are called the Early, Middle and Late Saxon periods. The Vikings also established themselves in parts of the country during this time.

Learning Objectives

- To understand that things change and to identify changes on a map.
- To identify clues from a picture source.
- To understand what an artefact is and to record observations about it.

Resource Page

Kings and Kingdoms
Both maps give basic information about different periods in Anglo-Saxon England and the children can compare the two. This introduces them to the idea that political maps change according to who holds power. (Please note that not all the kingdoms have been included, such as the Wreocensaete and the Magonsaete. Nor are the British kingdoms shown.) The power of the Anglo-Saxon kings fluctuated. Northumbria under Edwin (AD616–32) was powerful, as was Mercia under Ethelbald (AD716–57) and Offa (AD757–96), who built Offa's Dyke. However, it was Alfred the Great of Wessex who established England as a kingdom, along with his son Edward and grandson Athelstan. Discuss the term 'Danelaw', explaining that it was the part of Anglo-Saxon England administered by the Vikings in the ninth to eleventh centuries.

Using the Activity Pages

Sutton Hoo
Here the children are given an artist's impression of the Sutton Hoo Ship Burial. Though there were no remains of the actual ship, a clear impression was left. The precious objects suggest a warrior king (it is popularly thought to be the grave of Redwald, King of East Anglia). The children are asked to identify the grave, label the objects and make up kennings for them (this should include the ship). Kennings are a useful way of understanding the Anglo-Saxon values of pride and strength in battle, as well as their poetic nature. You may wish to explain that 'grave goods' were most likely intended for use in the afterlife.

Objects and Artefacts
This diagram can be used in conjunction with other enquiry or artefact sheets. It encourages the children to focus on recording details. It can be used in the classroom or on visits. The child should spend time accurately drawing the artefact or likeness in the centre of the sheet (for example, the Sutton Hoo helmet). Alternatively, images from photocopiable sheets could be pasted on. The children will need to know the term 'artefact'. Artefacts are often displayed in museums. Discuss with the children what they should put on the labels that accompany their artefacts.

Follow-up

- You can use either of the maps and compare them with a modern map of Britain. The children could try to identify what kingdoms some of today's major cities would have come under.
- The children could find out more about the Sutton Hoo treasure by locating information in libraries. They should try to identify particular artefacts. You may wish to use the Internet with the children or ask them to locate information themselves.

Kings and Kingdoms

- Look carefully at these two maps.

Some of the Main Anglo-Saxon Kingdoms about AD600

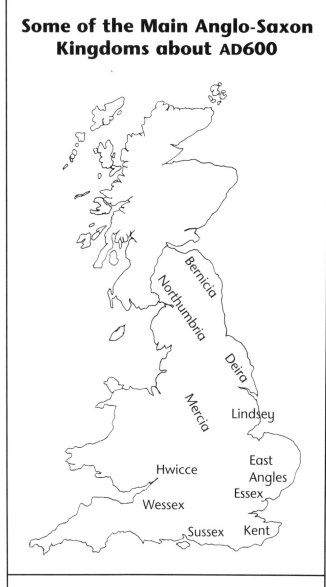

Key
- Essex – East Saxons
- Wessex – West Saxons
- Sussex – South Saxons

About AD900

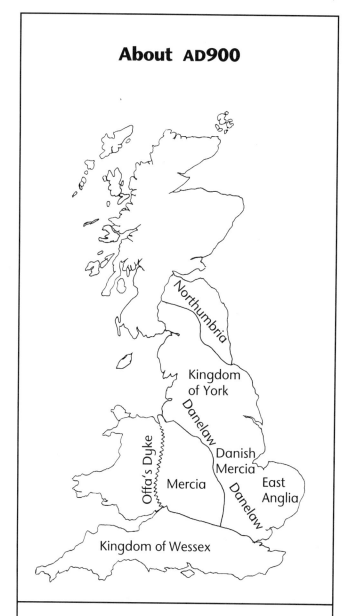

Notes
- Kingdom of York under Danelaw
- Alfred, King of Wessex, becomes king of the English
- Danelaw – the north and east were run by the Danes (Vikings)

Talking and Thinking
- What are these maps of?
- Which is the earlier map? Which is the later map? How do you know?
- List three major changes between the two maps.
- What do you think Offa's Dyke could be?

© Folens (copiable page)   History Highlights for Juniors 1   13

Sutton Hoo

At Sutton Hoo in Suffolk an Anglo-Saxon grave was discovered. It was very special. There were many objects (grave goods) found, but there was no body. Many people believe the grave was that of Redwald, King of East Anglia. He was a rich warrior king.

1. This is a picture of the grave without the objects. Marks were left in the sandy soil. What do the marks tell you about the grave? Write your answer by the picture.

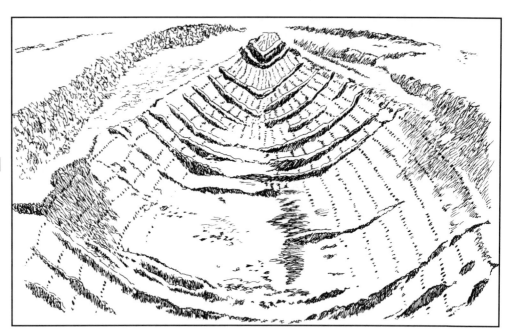

2. Below are some objects that are typical of those found in the grave. Label each object, using the words in the list.

- **helmet**
- **shield**
- **spear**
- **sword**
- **axe**
- **boar crest** (worn on the top of a helmet)

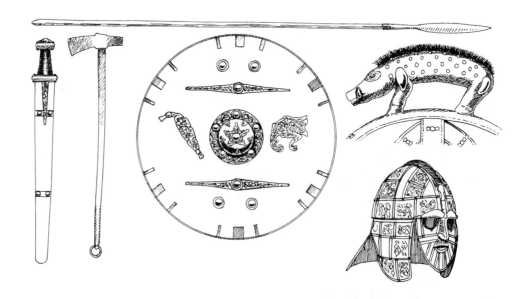

3. The Anglo-Saxons gave their ships and weapons names to describe how powerful they were. These names were called 'kennings'. For example, a kenning for a sword could be 'blood-spiller'! Think of kennings for all of the pictures on this page.

Objects and Artefacts

Name of artefact: _____

- Draw a picture of the artefact in the circle. Then fill in the boxes around it that are useful.

| **Where it was found** | **When it dates from** | **The design or detail** |

| **What it was made of** | **What it was used for** | **How it worked** |

Name: _____ Date: _____

ideas page

The Vikings

Background

The Vikings or Norsemen were highly skilled sailors, navigators, traders and craftspeople, who were also raiders and later became settlers. Between the eighth and eleventh centuries, they made lengthy voyages overseas, reaching places thousands of kilometres from Scandinavia and amassing considerable wealth as they did so. One of the earliest recorded raids was on the island of Lindisfarne in AD793. In addition, Vikings who had settled in one place might move to another. For example, it is thought that some Vikings who had settled in Ireland crossed to north-west England. Many modern place names, such as York and Grimsby, have their origins in Viking times.

Learning Objectives

- To locate the Viking homelands.
- To locate the routes taken by the Vikings and the countries settled.
- To understand the terms 'invade' and 'settle'.

Resource Page

Viking Sailors
The Resource Page focuses on the scope of the Viking journeys and includes the United Kingdom, Ireland, Scandinavia, Iceland and Europe on a modern world map. It indicates where the Vikings came from and the routes they are likely to have taken to reach Britain, Ireland and Iceland. The children will need to have a complete world map available to find other countries settled by the Vikings and to work out a probable route taken to Newfoundland (or Vinland as it was known). You may also wish to point out where Greenland is. Discuss the terms 'invade' and 'settle', and use the Resource Page to emphasise that Britain has always been settled by people from other countries, resulting in a rich language and culture. The map can be kept as a resource.

Using the Activity Pages

Viking Life
Here the children are asked to classify words associated with aspects of Viking settlers. However, to do this successfully, they need to separate them from irrelevant words associated with modern life, for example 'television'. The words vary in difficulty and the children may not be aware of some, such as 'saga' or 'mead'. They may also classify words correctly, but not understand their meanings. The Activity Page can therefore be an indication of the children's vocabulary and ability to place the Vikings historically. You can use their mistakes as the basis for teaching points later. The children can also add words to their lists. It will be helpful for the children to have access to dictionaries.

Reviewing My Work
This writing frame allows the children to consider what they already know, what they have learned, and what they would like to know more about and why. In the last paragraph, you may wish to encourage some children to write down what they do not understand.

Follow-up

- Point out to the children the evidence left by the Vikings in place names – 'by', for example, means a Viking farm or village. Point also to the way in which names might change, for example the Viking name for York was Jorvik.
- The children could find where Lindisfarne is and try to indicate where it should be on the map (it may also be called Holy Island on a modern-day map). They could also carry out an investigation into the attack on the Lindisfarne monastery, perhaps by using the Internet as well as the school library.
- If the children have seen any Viking re-enactments or festivals, these could be discussed with the class.

16

Viking Sailors

The Vikings came from what we now call Norway, Sweden and Denmark. They were expert sailors and travelled to many parts of the world.

Talking and Thinking
- Find where the Vikings came from.
- Follow the routes on the map. Where do they lead?
- Use a world map and find these places: Finland, France, Germany and Italy. Write them on the map (the map shows country borders as they exist today).
- Find Newfoundland on a world map. What route might the Vikings have taken to get there?

Viking Life

When the Vikings settled in a place, they built farms and homesteads.

- Look at this chart. Along the top it gives you a list of headings to do with Viking life. Choose words from the bottom of the page and write them under the correct headings.
- Be careful! Not all the words should be included.

tools and materials	food and drink	clothes and jewellery	transport	art, crafts and culture

meat   pasta   brooch   television   fish   saga   banana
flax   berries   oars   longship   cloak   nuts   dragon prow
anvil   cheese   car   axe   honey   ring   wood
tea   pendant   poem   boots   coffee   shoes
loom   wool   tapestry   tunic   mead   milk
water   leather   hammer   belt   bread   trousers

Reviewing My Work

- I already know some things about the Vikings. For example, I knew that

_____
_____
_____

and

_____
_____
_____

But I did not know

_____
_____

and I also did not know

_____
_____

I would like to know more about

_____
_____
_____

The reason for this is

_____
_____
_____

ideas page

Viking Ships

Background

The Vikings' ship-building skills allowed them to make successful expeditions, raiding not only along the coast, but also inland by travelling stealthily along the river systems. They were also successful traders and so the basic structure of the longship was adapted to suit different needs. It was made of oak and below the waterline there were overlapping planks, which allowed the boat to bend in rough waters. For support, it had a keel (a strip of wood along the bottom and running the length of the boat). It had a mast and sails that carried it faster when the wind was good, and a steering oar for guidance. There was also a crew of rowers.

Learning Objectives

- To understand what a Viking longship was and how it was instrumental in Viking expansion.
- To identify the longship's distinguishing features.
- To write about the voyage from a Viking sailor's point of view.

Resource Page

The Dragon Ship
Point out to the children how the boat was constructed and survived rough weather, noting also the covering that was used. Introduce words such as 'keel' and 'prow'. They should be able to deduce that the ship was driven by oars and wind, but point to the steering oar as being necessary and emphasise its usefulness when travelling along rivers and channels. The carved prow probably fulfilled several functions, including, perhaps, striking fear into the enemy. It may also have been regarded as some kind of talisman. Evidence of the dragon prow comes from such sources as ornaments and from illustrated monastic manuscripts.

Using the Activity Pages

The Oseberg Ship
The Oseberg ship was excavated in 1904 from a large burial mound in Vestfold, Norway. It had been built c.AD815–20, and had probably been used for pleasure before becoming a burial ship for a prominent woman and her handmaiden. In this activity, the children should apply what they have learned about ships to identifying aspects of the Oseberg ship. They should be able to recognise and label the keel, carved prow, mast, steering oar and placements for the oars, as well as noting that the boat is made of wooden planks. As far as possible, they should add explanatory comments, such as describing the purpose of the keel.

The Voyage
Here the children should write an imaginative account of a voyage from Denmark to Grimsby from a sailor's perspective. It should include a journey up the Humber estuary and along the River Ouse. They should try to use the work they have done about Viking expeditions and raids, referring to specific knowledge, such as the way the ship would be navigated upriver. They will need an atlas to plot their route before they begin.

Follow-up

- If possible, show the children illustrations or artefacts depicting the longships at sea and read descriptions of their arrival from the *Anglo-Saxon Chronicle*. The children can compare the differences and similarities and you can point out how historical depictions vary, explaining that building an accurate picture depends on reliable information which is not always available. Point out that there are some historical questions to which we do not have answers.
- Ask the children to carry out an investigation into the history of Viking York (Jorvik), using indexes and contents pages. It was an important market town.

The Dragon Ship

The Vikings used the longship to travel across the seas and up rivers. They raided villages and settlements. The prow (front part) of the ship had a carved and painted figurehead. These often looked like dragons or sea monsters. Those who saw these ships arriving for raids called them 'dragon ships'.

- Look at the longships below.

Talking and Thinking
- How is the Viking longship powered? Think of more than one way.
- How did the sailors shelter from rough weather?
- Why do you think the longship could travel up rivers? Think about other kinds of ships and boats you know and where they travel.
- Why do you think the longship had carved prows?
- No example of a dragon figurehead has been found. How do you think we know what they looked like?

The Oseberg Ship

Below is a picture of the Oseberg ship. This was found in Norway and was a burial ship. Skeletons were found in the boat. There was also furniture and other objects such as a bed and a cart. The Vikings believed that after death there was another world, so the dead were buried with their possessions.

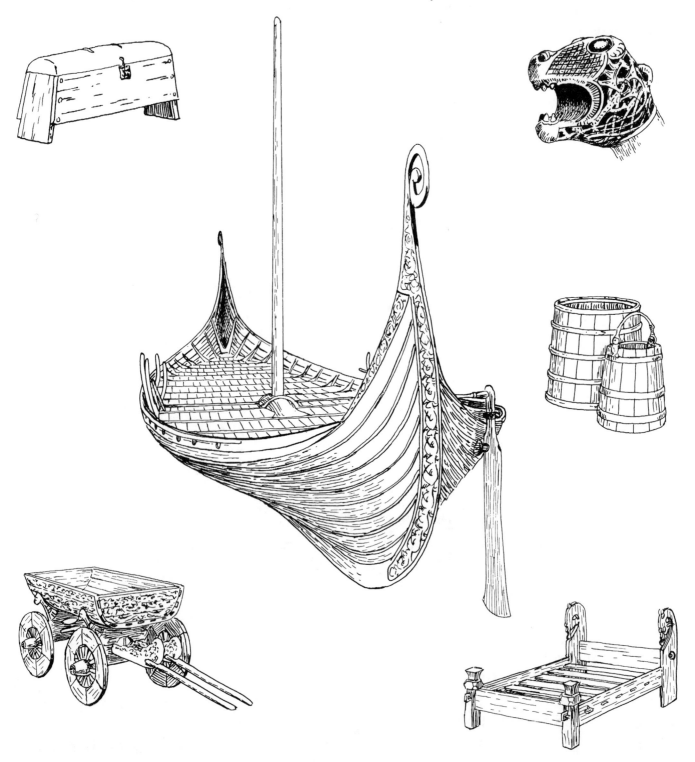

1. Using what you have learned, label as much of the Oseberg ship as you can.
2. Add extra information about each object.
3. Include a label saying what the ship was made of.

The Voyage

- Imagine that you are a Viking sailor setting out from Denmark to arrive in Grimsby. Grimsby was once a Viking settlement – 'by' means village or farm. You then travel up the River Ouse in your ship. You can be in a merchant ship or a warship.
- Use an atlas to find where the places are and to plot your route.
- Think about the work you have already done and answer these questions before you begin writing.

Starting Out
What is the purpose of your journey?

_____

Where will you begin your journey?

_____

How many are travelling with you?

_____

What will you carry with you?

_____

The Voyage
What is the weather like?

_____

How does the weather affect the ship and the sailors?

_____

Arriving
What happens at Grimsby?

_____

How does the ship get to the River Ouse from Grimsby?

_____

- Now write your account. Give yourself a Viking name!

ideas page

Rich Tudors

Background

This chapter can be used with the next.

Most houses of the type shown on the Resource Page were timber-framed with brick chimneys, and had tiled roofs and leaded windows. Despite the frequency of fire, many of these houses still stood a hundred years after being built, although extensions or modifications might have been made. Cheaper houses were built from brick or used less wood, especially towards the end of the sixteenth century when there was a timber shortage. Those belonging to the aristocracy would have galleries, mullioned windows, imposing staircases and courtyards, and might be built from sandstone or limestone.

Learning Objectives

- To identify some characteristics of Tudor houses.
- To explore how the lives of rich Tudors were more comfortable than those of the poor.
- To identify information from source material.

Resource Page

The Tudor House
This house would have belonged to a rich merchant and was built using wood, bricks and tiles. Some servants would have rooms in the garret. Provide useful words as necessary, for example shop, cellar, hall, chamber, garret, oak-panelled walls, pewter, wall hangings, tapestries. Help the children to locate the hall and talk about how its functions would have been very important in Tudor times. It was the main room in the house and would have been used for entertaining and business.

Using the Activity Pages

Comfort in Tudor Times
The children should discuss some of the developments that occurred in the houses of rich Tudors, for example windows with glass, deep fireplaces with ornate chimneys, the use of brick to replace wood and separate rooms for different purposes. They should also note the 'four-poster' beds with heavy curtains to keep out the cold. The children should use the blank outline of the rich Tudor house to talk about or write short notes discussing the purpose of each room shown. How were the rich Tudors very much more comfortable than their poor counterparts? They should think about the reasons for having such a lot of storage space for food and produce. Which of the rooms might still be found in modern houses and which might not now be needed?

The Tudor Kitchen
This example of a sixteenth-century kitchen is useful for encouraging close observation of source material by the children. They should note what foods are being cooked (such as the meat on a spit), as well as what utensils are used and by whom. They should also try to identify some of the produce that frames the picture. They should also note the presence of the cat and speculate about where it is (under the oven for warmth). These observations can form the basis of their questions.

Follow-up

- Following the work done on the Tudor house, ask the children to consider some of the similarities between modern living and the Tudor period. They should discuss the changes that double-glazing and central heating/closed fires have brought. Do modern houses still have chimneys? Do we still have living accommodation above shops?
- The children might explore some book or online resource material to extend their study of Tudor life, including famous Tudor houses such as Hampton Court.

The Tudor House

- Look at the picture below.

Talking and Thinking
- What kind of family would live in a house like this? Would they be rich or poor? How can you tell?
- How many storeys does the house have? What type of room is in each storey?
- What is the furniture like? What other items are in the rooms?
- Which is the most important room? What do you think it was used for?

Comfort in Tudor Times

- The rooms in the Tudor house below have been blanked out. What do you think each room would have been used for?

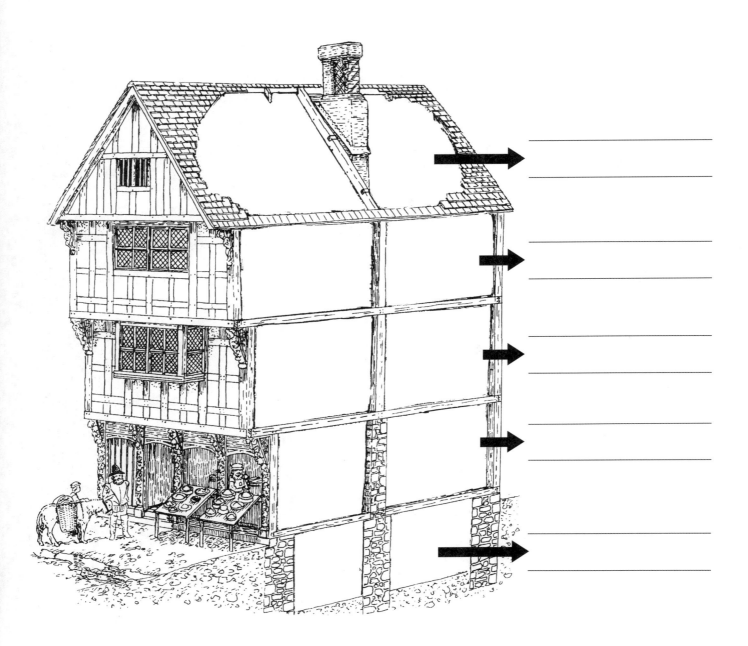

- Tick the rooms that you might find in a modern home.
- How did the Tudors make their homes comfortable and warm?
- How do we make our homes comfortable and warm?
- Are there any differences between Tudor houses and the houses of today?

The Tudor Kitchen

- Study this picture of a Tudor kitchen.

- Think about:
  - the people
  - the food
  - the utensils
  - the room
  - other interesting things.

- Now write six questions about the picture and give them to a partner to answer.
- Here is one to start you off:

  1. What are the people in the picture doing?

ideas page

Poor Tudors

Background

This chapter can be used with the previous one.

With the dissolution of the monasteries under Henry VIII, there was no one to help the poor. Although most beggars were vilified, a tax was levied to help those such as the sick and some almshouses were built from charitable money. The basic family homes of the country poor changed little from the medieval period to the Industrial Revolution. Even in the nineteenth century, country labourers were likely to live in one- or two-roomed houses similar to the hovels of the sixteenth century.

Learning Objectives

- To identify some characteristics of the hovel.
- To identify different attitudes to the poor.
- To identify information from source material.

Resource Page

The Hovel
The first illustration of the hovel shows a single-roomed dwelling, in which the whole family lived including any animals that were kept for produce and to sell at market. The animals would also provide some warmth when kept inside. The second illustration shows the structure of the home, which was made from wattle and daub. Some homes would have a second storey as sleeping quarters and storage. Fire would be one of the main hazards, as well as damp in winter. Rats in particular would carry disease.

Using the Activity Pages

The Beggar
There was a great fear of beggars, who were on the increase, in part due to land enclosure (land was fenced for sheep grazing and could not be farmed, thereby adding to unemployment). The source material here depicts a beggar being dragged through the streets. One figure is carrying a flail or whip. Others are watching or jeering. The children should note the person being hanged in the left-hand corner. Thousands were whipped or hung for begging or stealing. The nursery rhyme may date from the Tudor period; 'jags' is another name for rags and the velvet gown was likely to be a stolen one. You may wish to note if any children confuse 'jags' with the Jaguar car and use this error as a teaching point! See also *The Oxford Dictionary of Nursery Rhymes* edited by Iona and Peter Opie.

The Lives of the Poor
This writing frame should help the children to write coherently about the lives of the poor in Tudor times. The children can either complete the sheet or write out the starter sentences. They can also add further sentences and paragraphs comparing the lives of the poor with the rich.

Follow-up

- Ask the children to undertake some research and find out specific answers to:

    - why hovels had no glass windows
    - what an almshouse was
    - what the stocks were
    - what other names are used to describe beggars (such as 'vagabond' and 'vagrant').

    They can research origins in a dictionary.

The Hovel

- Look carefully at **A** and **B**.

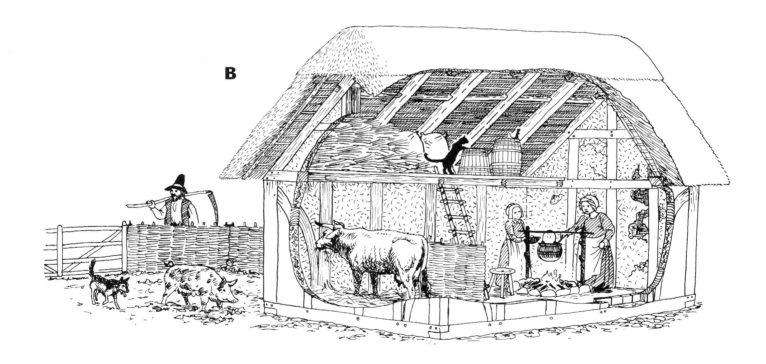

Talking and Thinking
- Who would live in a house like this? How can you tell?
- Why do you think people kept animals? Think of more than one reason.
- Why do you think some animals were kept inside?
- What was the house made of?
- What are the dangers of living in a house like this?
- What would the house be like to live in during the winter?

The Beggar

Men, women and children who had no work roamed through towns and villages looking for food or money. They became beggars and were treated badly by many people. However, some people believed that beggars who were old or sick should be helped and so gave money to charity.

- Look closely at the picture. Use the picture to answer these questions.

1. Which is the beggar? What is happening to him? What might happen to him?
2. What are the other groups of people doing?
3. Who are the rich? How can you tell?

- Read this nursery rhyme.

> *Hark, hark the dogs do bark,*
> *The beggars are coming to town;*
> *Some in rags, and some in jags,*
> *And some in velvet gowns.*

4. Write down why you think some beggars had velvet gowns.

- Now write down your answers to these questions.

5. Why do you think many beggars were treated badly?
6. How are attitudes to beggars today different, but also similar?

The Lives of the Poor

- Finish this writing frame. Use what you have learned.

In Tudor times some of the poor lived in

_____
_____

which were

_____
_____

Others were

_____
_____

You could become a beggar if

_____
_____

People had different attitudes towards beggars. For example

_____
_____

On the other hand

_____
_____

I think that the lives of the poor in Tudor times

_____
_____

ideas page

Henry VIII

Background

Henry VIII's life was profoundly affected by his overwhelming desire for a male heir. This was due to Tudor convention and also because of the recent prolonged period of civil war (the Wars of the Roses).

It was believed that kings would be stronger rulers and more able to unite the country than queens. Furthermore, a queen was likely to marry foreign royalty, which might mean another country could gain the English throne.

Learning Objectives

- To search for evidence in sources, compare sources and build a picture of Henry VIII.
- To recognise that people led different lives during the same historical period.
- To complete a timeline of Henry VIII, indicating his six wives.
- To understand some of the reasons why Henry VIII had several marriages.

Using the Activity Pages

Henry VIII's Timeline
The children can complete the timeline, beginning with Henry's birth. They can also answer the questions on the Activity Page and add information to it. The completed and correct timeline can be kept for future reference.

Henry VIII's Marriages
Here, the children are asked to consider several answers to the question 'Why did Henry marry so often?', and to tick the boxes 1–8 to show their choices. They are then asked to consider which two are the most important reasons (see points 4 and 8). The children can add further comments. For example, you might wish to point to some of the issues discussed in the background above.

Resource Page

Different Lives
The first illustration on the Resource Page shows Henry as a mature man and a monarch. The children should supply words to fit the image (for example, rich, powerful, kingly, frightening and so on). They could also describe the clothes he is wearing. (The doublet was worn by both sexes and most classes.) Alongside is an illustration of a Tudor farm worker. The children should compare the image with that of Henry. Point out that only the rich would have portraits painted and that these would be designed to flatter.

Follow-up

- Examples of Henry at different ages could be shown to the children. Ask them to point to both the similarities and the differences between them (for example, his facial characteristics are identifiable in all portraits).

Different Lives

A   B

Talking and Thinking
- Look at **A**.
- Who do you think it is a picture of?
- What does he seem like?
- What is he wearing?
- List words that describe what the picture tells you about him.

- Now look at **B**.
- What job does the person in this picture do? How can you tell?
- What is he wearing?
- In what ways are the two pictures different? List the differences on a chart like the one below.

Differences	
A	**B**

Henry VIII's Timeline

1. These dates are out of order. Mark them in order on Henry's timeline.

```
1491   Henry is born
1536   Marries Jane Seymour
1509   Henry becomes king and marries Catherine of Aragon
1543   Marries Catherine Parr
1547   Henry dies
1533   Marries Anne Boleyn
July 1540   Marries Catherine Howard
January 1540   Marries Anne of Cleves
```

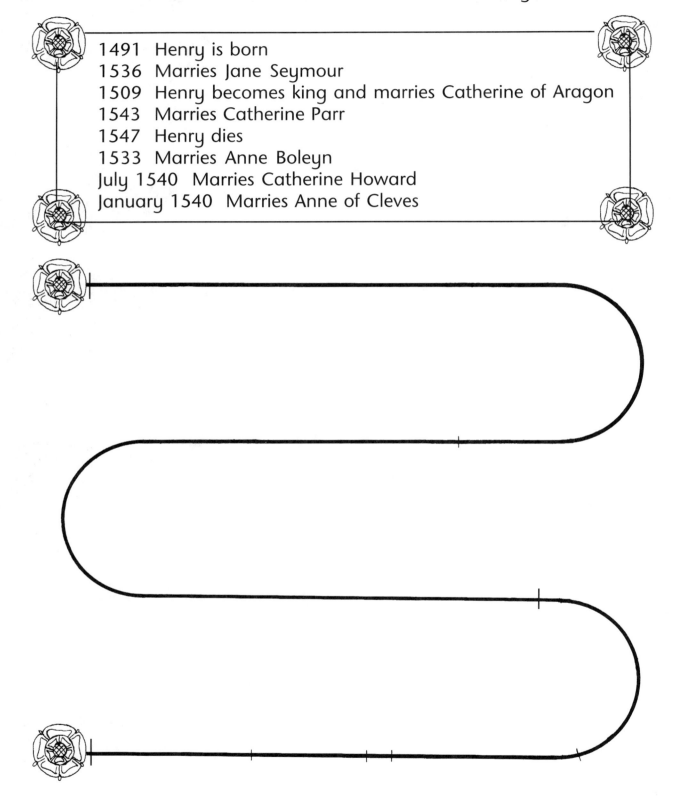

2. Find out which of Henry's wives were divorced by him, beheaded, died or survived him. Mark this information on the timeline.
3. How many children did Henry have? What were their names?
4. Who was Elizabeth I's mother?

Henry VIII's Marriages

- Why did Henry marry so often?

- Read all the comments.
  Then tick the boxes you agree with.

Catherine of Aragon   Anne Boleyn   Jane Seymour

Anne of Cleves

Catherine Howard

Catherine Parr

1. He wanted a daughter. ☐

2. He liked women. ☐

3. He kept falling in love. ☐

4. He wanted a son as his heir to the throne. ☐

5. The Pope agreed he could marry again. ☐

6. He wanted a large family. ☐

7. He thought he could do as he liked. ☐

8. He wanted to form pacts with other countries through marriage. ☐

- What do you think the two most important reasons are? ☐ ☐
  Put the numbers in the boxes.
- Can you think of any other reasons? Write your comments here.

_____

_____

_____

_____

_____

ideas page

The Second World War and the Home Front

Background

The illustration on the Resource Page is a primary source and comes from the children's section of *The Complete Home Entertainer*, published during the 1940s. The street scene depicts typical features from the war years, and the artist, Doreen Debenham, has used a graphic style popular at the time. There are up to 26 deliberate mistakes in the picture, which the children of the time would have been expected to identify – a game still found in quiz books today. The complete book contains a range of party games for adults and puzzles for children, all of which were popular before the advent of television. This is a period of history in which some of the children might have access to eye-witness information; this possibility could be explored with the class.

Learning Objectives

- To gain an understanding of how daily life changed during the war.
- To understand what air raids were and their consequences.
- To understand what kind of protection was offered and what protective measures people took themselves.

Resource Page

It's a Puzzle
Show the children the source material and ask them what they think it is for and what it depicts. Ask them what period they think it comes from and how they know. (Note the period car, bicycle and clothes, as well as the obvious indications of war.) You can reinforce the notion of historical change by pointing out that children today would not be able to identify all the deliberate mistakes. (For example, the woman talking to the soldier is carrying her gas mask upside down and the cinema attendant is wearing a bowler hat.)

Using the Activity Pages

Air Raid!
Not everyone recalled or experienced events in the same way. Here the children can compare sources and choose one as a model to write their own imaginative experience. Note whether they can identify what Bill Brandt's work is.

Taking Shelter
This page should be given out before the children have been told how an Anderson shelter functions, since they are asked to deduce this using both sources. In particular, their diagrams should reflect the corrugated sections as a shelter dug into the ground.

Follow-up

- There are many photographs depicting rationing, gas masks, women workers, the effects of air raids and the work of the ARP, and these could be used with the sources in this section in order to help children to build a picture of how the war affected civilians' daily lives.
- The Resource Page can also be used to discuss the ways in which the illustration does not suggest the period. For example, there is no evidence of bombing and in practice few people carried gas masks. Children might speculate about why the artist has chosen to present a well-ordered, obedient society.
- Discuss what the London Blitz was (*blitzkrieg*/lightning war) and the effects of the bombing on cities such as Coventry.

It's a Puzzle

Below is a picture from a book called *The Complete Home Entertainer*. It has lots of mistakes in it. Before you try to find them, complete the questions at the bottom of the page.

Talking and Thinking
- How can you tell the picture is not modern? Point to certain things.
- When do you think it was drawn? Again, what clues tell you? Find at least three.
- Now find as many of the deliberate mistakes in the picture as you can.

© Folens (copiable page)   History Highlights for Juniors 1   37

Air Raid!

On 7 September 1940, during the Second World War, night-time bombing of major towns and cities began. 430 people were killed and there were over 1,500 casualties. Bombing of this kind continued until the end of December.

1. Read **A** and **B** below.

A

> And as I watched the houses drain themselves of people, like water down a sink, and as the dull vibrating noise of planes became audible in the distance I knew it was real ... I saw how cheap, how frail our life is. Just a puff, and a life, perhaps of a great man or an ordinary person who liked his pint of beer and his pipe, was snuffed out, for ever, just like that.
>
> from *Boy in the Blitz* by Colin Perry

B

> Under the soft light of the moon the blacked-out town had a new beauty. The houses looked flat like painted scenery and the bombed ruins made strangely shaped silhouettes.
>
> Bill Brandt, *War Work*, The Photographer's Gallery

2. Write short notes in the table below comparing **A** and **B**. Say:
  – what you think is happening
  – how each person feels about war in the city.

A	B

3. Now choose one source as a model to write your own commentary, as though you were there.

Taking Shelter

When an air raid began not everybody left their homes. Some crouched under the stairs or a table. In London, many people found safety in the underground railways. Others took refuge in their Anderson shelters.

1. Look carefully at **A** and read **B**.

A

B

> The government didn't *build* shelters for you. Council workmen just came with a lorry and dumped the bits on your front lawn and left you to get on with it. We didn't think much of the bits, lying out in the rain gathering rainwater. Just thin bits of corrugated iron, like some shed. People felt they'd be safer in their houses, solid bricks and mortar. They weren't going out in the middle of the night to bury themselves in a grave.
>
> Then my father saw an Anderson that had received a direct hit; he said there was quite a lot of it left; the house it had belonged to was just a heap of bricks.
>
> from *Children of the Blitz* by Robert Westall

2. Work out how and where people built their Anderson shelters.
3. Draw diagrams to explain.
4. Write down why you think the shelters were safer than staying in the house.

ideas page

The Second World War: Evacuation

Background

Evacuation during the Second World War was a varied experience. There were those who were lucky enough to be housed with caring, well-adjusted families, while others suffered neglect and, at the worst, abuse. Some felt abandoned. Others enjoyed the new experience. For most, being separated from parents at a young age created mixed feelings not likely to be forgotten.

Learning Objectives

- To understand what evacuation was.
- To understand that evacuation was not experienced in the same way by everyone.
- To understand what an eye-witness account is.

Using the Activity Pages

What's Happening?
This page involves role-play. As interviewers, the children should ask questions pertinent to evacuation.
For example: 'Why are you at the railway station?'; 'Why are you being evacuated?' They should also take on the role of the evacuee by answering a partner's questions.

A Message for Home
The children are asked to empathise with the experience of the evacuee and should already have some general knowledge of this. They are asked to create a card and letter to be sent home, which should depict their circumstances. The children will therefore need to adopt a persona reflecting the evacuee's attitude to his or her circumstances. They can refer to the Resource Page for help here.

Resource Page

Saying Goodbye
Ask the children to read both of the sources. Referring to the first two points on the page discuss what is happening, emphasising the large numbers of children who were evacuated (approximately 250,000 from London on the first day alone). Note also that hospital patients, for example, were evacuated.

Discuss the different perspectives given of the same event in the sources. Point to the source information and date. The children should be clear that these are eye-witness accounts (though they have been recorded many years after the event). Both these sources come from *The Evacuation: the true story*, by Martin Parsons and Penny Starns.

Follow-up

- Ask the children to research evacuation by looking at personal testimony in a range of suitable books (for example, see *The Evacuation*, the personal account mentioned in 'Saying Goodbye'). Others might read one of the fictional accounts of evacuation, for example *Carrie's War* by Nina Bawden. Working in pairs, they can amass a selection of contrasting comments giving a different account of evacuation. These can be discussed in groups.
- The children might also collect personal first-hand accounts from relatives or members of their local community who may have recollections of being evacuated, although this may need to be dealt with sensitively. They can develop the work already done. According to the children's ability, you may first wish to discuss the difference between open and closed questions.

Saying Goodbye

In September 1939 children were moved out of the cities to safer places, if parents agreed. This was called 'evacuation'. Most of the children affected (evacuees) were city children who were sent to the countryside to live with strangers.

A

'That day I remember was one of shouting. Porters shouting at us, teachers shouting at us. At Queens Road Station it was "Keep back from the edge, keep back from the edge!" Nobody knew where we were going, our parents didn't know. I was wildly excited, people were watching us go, the streets were lined with people and I thought it was marvellous. What I didn't understand was why so many of the women and older girls were crying.'

James Roffey remembering evacuation, 1939

B

'It was terribly tearful, it was heart-rending really. They were babies really, five-year olds, four-year olds. It was terribly sad.'

Brenda Evans remembering evacuation, 1939

Talking and Thinking
- Why do you think it was city children who were evacuated? What other people from the cities were evacuated?
- Read **A** again. Where do you think the events are taking place? Why?
- Read **B** again. How are these memories different from those in **A**?
- **A** and **B** are eye-witness accounts. What does this mean?

What's Happening?

- Imagine you are an interviewer. Children are gathered together to be evacuated. You are going to ask one of them questions about what is happening.

1. Finish these questions.

Why _____

Where _____

When _____

How _____

Who _____

2. Write down three more questions to ask.

(a) _____

(b) _____

(c) _____

3. Ask a partner to answer your questions. They will have to pretend they are an evacuee.

A Message for Home

1. It is 1939. Imagine you have just been evacuated to the countryside. Your mum is at home in the city and it is her birthday. You have no money to buy her a present, but you are going to make her a special birthday card.

   - The card should show how your life in the countryside is different from your mum's in the city.
   - Make up a greeting that shows her birthday is during the war.

2. You are going to include a letter for your mum with the card. In it, you should write about what your life is like as an evacuee. It might be happy or sad, or both.
   - Below make notes about what you will include.

Where you are staying.	What is new about the countryside.
Who is looking after you and what they are like.	Whether you are with any other evacuees and if so what they are like.

3. Now write your letter. Remember to include a make-believe address from the countryside.

ideas page

Ancient Egypt

Background

The Nile is the heart of Egypt and was crucial in the development of agriculture. Its yearly floods turned arid land into fertile soil, providing a rich food supply.

Other aspects of the Ancient Egyptian culture were then able to develop.

Learning Objectives

- To locate Egypt and the Nile on a map.
- To understand the importance of the Nile and why agriculture developed.
- To understand aspects of farming in Ancient Egypt and compare this with modern developments.
- To make deductions by observing pictures of source material.

Resource Page

The Nile

Ask the children to study the map and the course of the Nile and discuss the questions with them. They should deduce that:

- the yearly floods create fertile soil, which allows agriculture to develop
- the fertile soil runs alongside the course of the river
- without the yearly floods famine would ensue
- the Nile provided water, fish and a means of transport.

Using the Activity Pages

Working the Land

The order of the illustrations and captions is: 1. Ploughing; 2. Sowing; 3. Cutting the corn; 4. Threshing; 5. Winnowing. Other related jobs included recording the amount of grain stored in the granary. This was carried out by educated scribes. The children also need to deduce that in B, jars are being used to measure such produce as grain or wine, and scales are being used for other goods, in order to pay taxes. Clues are given in the introduction at the top of the page (see also 'Follow-up' below).

What Can It Tell You?

This Activity Page depicts pottery making. It comes from a wall painting in the tomb of Beni Hassan. The first series of pictures illustrates the potter at his wheel creating different kinds of clay pots. In the second series the fire is being stoked, the pots baked and being carried away in baskets. It is thought that the Egyptians may have been among the first to devise the potter's wheel.

Follow-up

- Discuss the building of the Aswan Dam, which creates a regular flow of water all year round and also produces electricity, and ask the children to compare Ancient Egyptian farming with modern farming. They could look at what has changed (for example, crops are now grown throughout the year), and what has remained the same (the importance of the Nile to agriculture).
- You could also discuss the negative aspects of the dam: the destruction of villages and ancient monuments.
- The illustration B in 'Working the Land' is based on an illustration from *Man Must Measure The Wonderful World of Mathematics* by Lancelot Hogben. You may wish to point to it as an example of a secondary source.

44

The Nile

The River Nile was very important to the Ancient Egyptians. Most years there were heavy rains in East Africa which then flowed down the Nile and flooded the land along the river. This helped to create rich, fertile soil in an area of desert.

- Look at the map carefully.

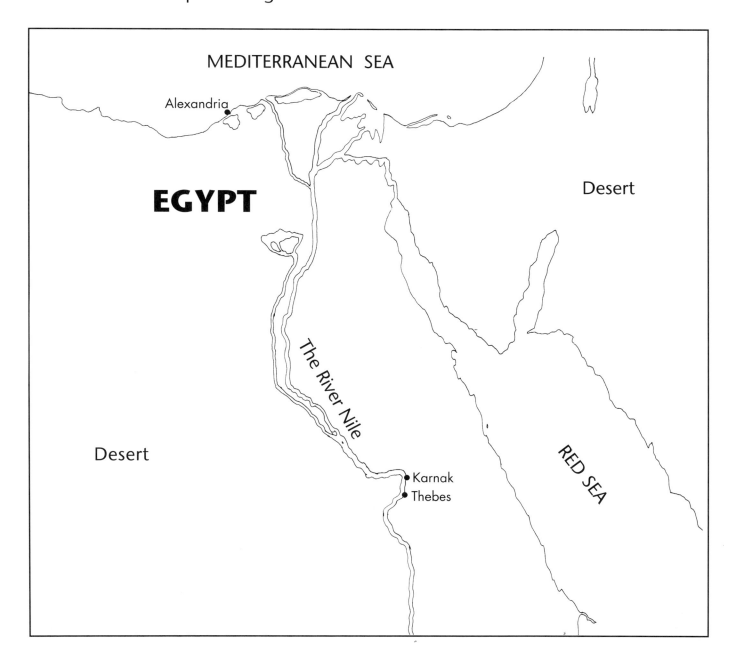

- Now answer these questions.

1. What important event happened to the Nile most years? What did this do?
2. Where do you think the Egyptians grew crops? Mark the area on the map.
3. What would happen if there was too little rain?
4. In what other ways was the Nile useful?

Working the Land

The Ancient Egyptians grew crops in the rich soil along the River Nile. They did different farming jobs. At harvest, taxes were paid in grain or other goods, not in money. Standard measurements were used to do this.

1. Look at **A** below. These pictures are not in the correct order.
2. Match the correct caption to each picture by drawing a line from the caption to the picture.
3. Now number the pictures 1 to 5 to show the order in which they happened.

A

1. Ploughing with oxen.
2. Sowing the seeds.
3. Cutting the ripe corn.
4. Threshing or beating down the corn with oxen to separate the grain from the husks.
5. Winnowing or throwing the grain in the air so the wind will blow away the husks.

After the grain had been threshed and winnowed, it was taken away to store.

4. Look at **B**.
   What do you think is happening? Why?
   Write a caption to explain.

_____

_____

B

46   History Highlights for Juniors 1   © Folens (copiable page)

What Can It Tell You?

The Ancient Egyptians were skilled at many crafts.

- Look carefully at the pictures below. They are based on a wall painting.
- What is going on in the pictures? Explain by writing some sentences under each section.

Coverage of the QCA Scheme of Work for Key Stages 1 and 2

Unit 1 (Yr 1) How were our toys different from those in the past? *History for Infants Chapters 1 & 2*	**Unit 2 (Yr 1)** What were homes like long ago? *History for Infants Chapters 3 & 4*	**Unit 3 (Yrs 1–2)** What were seaside holidays like in the past? *History for Infants Chapters 5 & 6*	**Unit 4 (Yr 2)** Why do we remember Florence Nightingale? *History for Infants Chapters 7 & 8*
Unit 5 (Yr 2) How do we know about the Great Fire of London? *History for Infants Chapters 9, 10 & 11*	**Unit 6 (Yrs 3–4)** Why have people invaded and settled in Britain in the past? *History for Juniors 1 Chapters 1–5*	**Unit 7 (Yrs 3–4)** Why did Henry VIII marry six times? *History for Juniors 1 Chapter 8*	**Unit 8 (Yrs 3–4)** What were the differences between the lives of rich and poor people in Tudor times? *History for Juniors 1 Chapters 6 & 7*
Unit 9 (Yrs 3–4) What was it like for children in the Second World War? *History for Juniors 1 Chapters 9 & 10*	**Unit 10 (Yrs 3–4)** What can we find out about Ancient Egypt from what has survived? *History for Juniors 1 Chapter 11*	**Unit 11 (Yrs 5–6)** What was it like for children living in Victorian Britain? *History for Juniors 2 Chapters 1 & 2*	**Unit 12 (Yrs 5–6)** How did life change in our locality in Victorian times?
Unit 13 (Yrs 5–6) How has life in Britain changed since 1948? *History for Juniors 2 Chapters 3 & 4*	**Unit 14 (Yrs 5–6)** Who were the Ancient Greeks? *History for Juniors 2 – Chapter 5*	**Unit 15 (Yrs 5–6)** How do we use Greek ideas today? *History for Juniors 2 Chapters 6 & 7*	**Unit 16 (Yrs 5–6)** How can we find out about Indus Valley civilisations? *History for Juniors 2 Chapter 8*
Unit 17 (Yr 2) What are we remembering on Remembrance Day?	**Unit 18 (Yrs 3–4)** What was it like to live here in the past?	**Unit 19 (Yrs 5–6)** What were the effects of Tudor exploration? *History for Juniors 2 Chapters 9 & 10*	**Unit 20 (Yrs 5–6)** What can we learn about recent history from studying the life of a famous person? *History for Juniors 2 Chapter 11*